DOLLS

Discover the most popular dolls of all time!

DOLLS

An inside look at dolls from Raggedy Ann ™ to Barbie ™

by Vivian Werner
Illustrated by Julie Durrell

AN AVON CAMELOT BOOK

A Byron Preiss Book

For Beverley, Lisa and Annie—*V.W.*

DOLLS is an original publication of Avon Books.
This work has never before appeared in book form.

AVON BOOKS
A division of
The Hearst Corporation
105 Madison Avenue
New York, New York 10016

Special thanks to Ellen Krieger, our editor at Avon Books

Editors: Ruth Ashby, Gillian Bucky
Photo Researcher: Laura Wolner
Book design by Anne Scatto
Cover design by Stephen Brenninkmeyer
Front cover photograph by Ben Asen
Raggedy Ann & Andy Copyright © 1990
Macmillan, Inc. All Rights Reserved.
Barbie Copyright © 1989 Mattel, Inc.

Editorial consultant: Rebekah Montgomery

Library of Congress Cataloging in Publication Data:
Werner, Vivian L.
  Dolls / by Vivian Werner ; illustrated by Julie Durrell.
    p.   cm. (An Avon Camelot book) "A Byron Preiss book."
  Summary: Examines dolls down through the ages, including those of the ancient Egyptians,
medieval Europe, and the twentieth century.
1. Dolls—History—Juvenile literature. [1. Dolls—History.] I. Durrell, Julie, ill.   II. Title.
NK4894.A2W43   1991   90-21077
688.7'221'09—dc20   AC

First Avon Camelot Printing: January 1991

"Camelot World" is a trademark of Byron Preiss Visual Publications, Inc.

CAMELOT TRADEMARK REG. U.S. PAT. OFF. AND IN OTHER
COUNTRIES, MARCA REGISTRADA, HECHO EN U.S.A.

Printed in the U.S.A.

OPM   10   9   8   7   6   5   4   3   2   1

CONTENTS

Barbie is the most successful doll of all time. Many other dolls from very different civilizations and cultures came before her.

IN THE BEGINNING

The holiday season is coming. The ground is white with snow and the trees are bright with sparkling lights. The spicy fragrance of gingerbread, freshly baked, fills the air.

The window of the toy shop is crammed full. There are tiny, shiny trains here, bats and balls and boxes of blocks there. Best of all, the shelves are lined with dolls.

There are baby dolls and Barbie dolls and dolls dressed as ballerinas. There are white dolls and black dolls and Oriental dolls. There are soldiers and sailors and astronauts. All of them are toys—playthings for children.

DOLLS

Most of these dolls are realistic. They look very much like the children who will play with them. And they're a far cry from the earliest dolls known.

Those first dolls were made by primitive people, as long as 25,000 years ago. They were made of clay, and they were crudely formed. Their heads and bodies were just blobs; their arms and legs were little more than stumps. Yet they were clearly modeled in the image of human beings.

The primitive people who made these dolls never thought of them as humans, though. Instead they thought that the dolls were gods. They believed that the dolls controlled the rising and setting of the sun and that they caused storms. They even believed that the dolls could ward off evil.

Because the dolls seemed to work such magic, only the oldest and wisest members of these people's tribes were allowed to handle them. Sorcerers used the dolls for sacred ceremonies; medicine men used them in healing rites. But children were never allowed to touch them. Many thousands of years would pass before people came to regard dolls as toys and gave them to children to play with.

IN THE BEGINNING

The very first people to give dolls as toys to children were the Egyptians, about 3,000 years before the Christian Era. Their earliest dolls were crude, although they were far more polished than those made by primitive peoples. Some were made of linen stuffed with papyrus. Most, though, were made of clay or of wood. Some of these primitive dolls even had "hair" made of strands of linen or of beads strung together.

But later dolls had real hair, as well as arms and legs that could be moved. Almost all were dolls of women or girls. There was also a crocodile doll that opened and closed his mouth. He appears to have been a great favorite.

The Egyptians also used dolls for another purpose. They placed them in the graves of those who had died. It was the custom among the Egyptians to bury food, clothes, and household goods alongside the dead. They reasoned that the dead would need these items in the afterworld.

If the dead had been wealthy, they would also need servants. If they had been landowners, they would need slaves to work their fields. And they would need both servants and slaves to accompany them on their journeys to the spirit world.

For a long time, actual slaves and servants were buried alongside their masters. Gradually, the Egyptians replaced real people with dolls.

The dolls were called *Ushabti* and were made of clay, stone, wood, or even alabaster. The earliest ones were made to look like mummies. Their bodies were tightly wrapped and only their faces showed. Later ones, though, looked more like living beings. Some were very beautiful and very elaborate.

Egyptian Ushabti figurines were buried alongside people who had died.

Among the most remarkable were the Ushabti found in the tomb of a very wealthy and important man named Mehenkwetre. He was a chancellor and steward at the royal palace of King Mentohotep III and he lived about 2,000 B.C.

The Ushabti found in Mehenkwetre's tomb were arranged in 24 different groups. Each group depicted a scene from life on a gentleman's country estate. (Some of these dolls are now on display at the Metropolitan Museum of Art in New York City.)

In one scene, showing how bread was made, women slaves grind the corn, and men make the dough into tiny cakes. In another, men work in a vegetable garden. In still another, they work in a carpenter shop. Scenes show women spinning and weaving; girls carrying baskets of bread and wine. In short, these doll scenes depicted all the household tasks being carried out.

Mehenkwetre himself appears in some of these groups. Sometimes he is at work, as when he sits in his courtyard and counts his cattle. More often he is on a boat. Then he sits on a chair and peacefully smells a lotus blossom while his slaves row or hoist the sails.

About 1,000 years later, and not too far away,

another civilization flourished. It was that of ancient Greece and there, too, dolls were popular. Small clay dolls were sold everywhere: in the shops, in the market place, even on street corners. They were so inexpensive that almost every child could have one. Many of these dolls had moveable arms and legs.

The girls in Greece played with dolls until they were 13 or 14. It was at that age that they married. When that time came, the girls offered their dolls to one of the two goddesses who protected women. It could be Artemis, the

goddess of the hunt. Or it could be Aphrodite, the goddess of beauty. Boys who played with dolls—and many did—left their dolls to Apollo, the sun-god.

After a while, the Greek civilization gave way to the Roman. In that era, too, dolls were common. In Rome it was the custom to give them to little girls during the Saturnalia, the yearly festival dedicated to Saturn, the god of harvests.

Like the Grecian girls, the Romans played with their dolls until it was time for them to marry. Then they, too, dedicated their dolls to the gods. In the early days of the Roman Empire, the gods to whom the dolls were given were the two gods of the household, Lares and Penates. Later the young girls dedicated the dolls to Venus, the goddess of love.

Dolls were important and had religious significance in the Far East, as well. At one time, both the Chinese and the Japanese considered dolls sacred. That was several thousand years ago. Later, popular dolls in each country celebrated great religious leaders.

In China, that leader was Buddha, the teacher who founded the religion most Chinese practice. According to Chinese tradition, Buddha cannot fall.

The doll inspired by Buddha is called the "tilting doll." It's a simple figure cut from cardboard or stiffened paper. It has two sticks for a body. The bottom is weighted, and the doll is so carefully balanced that, like Buddha, it cannot fall.

The Japanese doll is called the *Daruma* doll, named for the Buddhist priest who founded the sect known as Zen. Because Daruma sat for nine years on a rock without moving, the doll has no feet. Like the tilting doll, it is weighted and never falls.

Christians have never worshiped dolls. But in Catholic churches, statues are displayed on festive occasions.

In many European countries, a *crèche* is set out at Christmastime in churches and cathedrals, as well as in homes. This is a group of figures that represents the Nativity, the birth of Jesus.

The Infant lies in a manger, while Joseph and Mary stand beside it. These figures are as realistic as possible. With them are the Three Kings and their attendants, dressed in splendid robes. There are animals, too: oxen and asses and sometimes lambs. These

Japanese Daruma dolls are weighted so that they cannot tip over.

animals may be watched over by shepherds, whose clothing—in contrast to that of the Kings—is very simple.

The crèche is traditional in France, Germany, Austria, and especially in Italy. Other statues of the Virgin Mary are also brought out for church festivals in those countries.

Such statues, though, have not been allowed

in Protestant churches. In the 16th century, a man named Martin Luther led people to rise up against the vast show of wealth in the Catholic Church. The result was the founding of Protestant churches. Protestants banned all but the simplest music. They outlawed the rich robes of the priests. And they saw to it that the statues that had stood near the altars were removed.

This movement began in Germany and spread to other countries, including England. There, too, the statues were stripped from the churches. In other countries such statues were destroyed, but in England they were given to children to play with. English children have loved dolls ever since.

For the most part and in most places, people stopped worshiping dolls as gods nearly 2,000 years ago. Yet the custom persisted until recently among the Hopi Indians of North America. These people worshiped hundreds of spirits, who represented such natural elements as the earth,

In many countries, crèches are a familiar sight at Christmastime.

the sky, the warm wind, and the soft rain. These spirits were called *kachinas*.

To impersonate these spirits for their ritual dances, the Hopi painted their faces. They put on masks and fantastic feathered headdresses, too. They also made a doll for each spirit; each doll was the exact image of one of the painted braves.

The dolls were called kachinas, like the spirits. The Hopi worshiped them, just as they worshiped the spirits, and used them in the ceremonies. When the ceremonies were over, though, the dolls were given to the children, both to teach them about their traditions and to play with.

Even today, there are some places where dolls are considered magic. These are in the parts of West

Hopi Indians used kachina figures in their ritual dances.

12

Africa and the nations of the West Indies where people practice voodoo, a religion based on African forms of worship. In voodoo, spells can be cast by sticking a doll with pins. This is supposed to cause pain to the person the doll represents. Sometimes a wax doll is melted, to bring death to the person it represents.

By and large, though, dolls are simply the favorite toy of children everywhere. Whether they're rag dolls or dolls of finest porcelain, they are loved and cherished by the little girls and boys who own them.

Fashion dolls, such as this pair from around 1870, displayed the latest styles of dress.

2

CENTURIES
LATÉR

The French call a doll *poupée*. The Germans call it *Puppe*. And the word *puppet* is common in English.

All three words come from the Latin word *pupa*. That means newborn. But baby dolls were almost unknown until about 100 years ago, and neither the French nor the Germans thought of dolls as infants. Instead, they thought of them as very small adults.

The French, especially, were known for their dolls. French dolls were so beautifully made and so exquisitely dressed that they were truly fit for a queen. And so it became a tradition to

15

make gifts of them to members of royal families.

This custom started with Charles VI, who ruled France from 1380 until 1422. It began when he gave a collection of dolls to the queen of England.

But these dolls were not toys. Instead they were fashion dolls, with clothes in the very latest style. Their meaurements were in proportion to the queen's own measurements. Their robes were stitched by the king's own tailor. And their clothes were copies of those

introduced to the French court by Isabeau of Bavaria, the bride of Charles.

A century later, Anne of Brittany, the wife of King Charles VIII, gave a doll to Queen Isabella of Spain. It was Isabella who supposedly pawned her jewels to pay for the voyage of Christopher Columbus to the New World. During her lifetime, though, she was best known for the elegance of her dress.

Isabella was a vain woman. She spent much of her time choosing her gowns, then more time choosing the accessories. Everything, even the handkerchief she trailed from her hand, had to match. So a large doll was made for Isabella and dressed in the height of fashion. Her clothes were of the finest French workmanship. But when the doll was finished, it was decided that she was far too plain for the Spanish queen.

Another doll was made. Once more it was decided that the doll was too plain, that her clothes were not elegant enough, that she would never please the fussy Isabella. Finally, a third doll was considered suitable for Isabella.

The Italian Marie de Medici, who would become queen of France, was far easier to please.

At the time she was engaged to marry Henry IV of France, Marie wrote to him and asked for samples of French fashions. He quickly had some model dolls sent to her in Florence. They were dressed in the latest styles.

Henry's gift was meant to show Marie the wealth and refinement of the French court. It was meant to provide her with patterns for her own robes and gowns. And it was also meant to please the bride-to-be.

It must have done so because Marie continued to collect fashion dolls as long as she lived. After Henry was assassinated, in 1610, she had 16 of them dressed in deepest mourning, to show her respect for the king.

Louis XIII was the son of Marie and Henry. Although Marie had dolls to display fashions, Louis's dolls were playthings.

Louis was only nine years old when Henry was assassinated. Nevertheless, as Henry's rightful heir, he ascended the throne. But he was far too young to rule. That was left to his mother and her advisors. So the small boy played with his toys.

Among these were two little marmosets, a kind of monkey. They were made of china. A third marmoset rode on the back of a horse and held two greyhounds by their leash. Louis had a doll gorgeously dressed as a young gentleman. Other dolls represented older people. Still another, a china doll, was dressed like a monk. Besides those, he had some little angels playing the flute or bagpipes. There was a tiny coach, too. It was jam-packed with tiny dolls.

Louis XIV, the son of Louis XIII, also played with dolls. He was one of the greatest of all French kings. Eventually he became known for the brilliance of his court at Versailles, where he built a magnificent chateau. But Louis XIV

A portrait of Louis XIV as a child.

was only five years old in 1643, when he became king. Like his father before him, he was too young to rule. So his mother served as his regent, or agent, just as his grandmother had served Louis XIII. All the while the tiny boy who wore the crown played happily with his toys.

And what marvelous toys they were! Louis had two little Moors playing a flute and a trumpet. The figures were only three and a half inches long, and they lay on a bed of silver filigree, silver so delicately worked that it might have been lace. Louis had an especially beautiful house for his dolls, and two little theaters as well. These were made of wood. Both were painted blue and decorated with silver filigree. Many years later, when Louis had a real theater built in his palace at Versailles, it was painted blue, too, and decorated with silver.

Besides his dollhouse and theater, the little Louis XIV had nine markets and shops. Each was complete with tiny enamel figures. He had a toy gardener, too, with a toy wheelbarrow, and a toy knife grinder with a toy wheel. The little king even had a miniature sedan chair, with lackeys to carry it.

QUEEN MARY'S DOLLHOUSE

Probably the most fabulous dollhouse ever built was a gift of the English people to their queen, Mary, the wife of King George V, as an expression of their affection.

The house, built in the 1920s, is complete in every detail. It has both hot and cold running water that flows from tiny taps. Its splendid rooms are lit by electricity. It boasts two working elevators, one for the family, the other for the servants.

The furniture in the first-floor formal rooms is faithfully copied from 18th-century styles. It is upholstered in fabrics of the period, made to a miniature scale.

Portraits of the king and queen hang on the wall of one room. Beneath them is a grand piano. Its keys and pedals work, although it is less than a foot long.

Books in the library are leather bound and only one inch high. They were written, and often signed, by England's most important writers.

The walnut table in the dining room is set with silver plates, not much larger than a quarter. A lovely china service, with the Queen's own crest on each tiny plate, is displayed on a sideboard.

The kitchen, just off the dining room, is equipped with a battery of copper pots. Each is lined with tin, like those used in the royal kitchen.

*A detail of Queen Mary's dollhouse showing the
drawing room (top) and dining room (bottom).*

The king's bedroom in Queen Mary's dollhouse.

Bedrooms are on the floors above. That of the queen has walls hung with damask. There are the tiniest of brushes and combs and powder boxes on the little vanity table that is itself only a few inches high. There is a tiny silver inkwell and a tiny picture of Queen Victoria on the little walnut writing table.

The bedroom of the Princess Royal is simpler than that of the queen. But, in fairy-tale tradition, there is the very tiniest of peas beneath the mattress.

This wondrous house boasts a wine cellar, stocked with miniature bottles filled with the finest champagnes and clarets and brandies. Another cellar, just as well stocked, is for groceries.

Like a proper English house, the dollhouse has a garden beside it. Miniature flowers bloom there all year round. Tiny birds nest in trees and guard their eggs. Even tinier snails curl up on little leaves.

On the other side of the house is the garage. There are six miniature motor cars there. One is a Rolls-Royce, and two are Daimlers. Truly, Queen Mary's dollhouse—along with everything in it—is fit for a queen.

Around this time a passion for dolls developed in Paris. Many elegant women owned a pair of them. Of this pair, one was called the "Grande Pandore," and she was magnificently dressed. Her gown was the latest design, and her hair was elaborately arranged. She often wore splendid, but miniature, jewels. She most certainly carried the accessories every woman of fashion carried: the tiniest of ivory fans, long kid gloves, and a little beaded reticule, or handbag.

The other doll was known as the "Petite Pandore," and she was "en déshabillé." That's the French word for undressed. It meant that the doll was used to display underthings from corsets and camisoles to pantaloons and petticoats.

Things were changing now in Europe. Wars had been fought and won. Wars had been fought and lost, as well. And all across the Continent new courts were springing up.

They were small courts and would never match the wealth or power of those of England and France and Spain. But the rulers of those courts and their advisers and attendants were eager to follow the customs of the larger courts. Above all, their ladies longed to be as fashionable as the ladies of France.

Only a few could travel to France to see for

This French Grande Pandore dates from 1770-1775.

themselves what was being worn there. But like Marie de Medici, they could ask that fashion dolls be sent to them.

Before long, wealthy women who were not of noble birth were also sending to Paris for fashion dolls. Soon a whole new industry sprang up in that city. It occupied many streets in one section; it employed a large number of tailors and seamstresses, as well as designers. It was a fashion industry, but the fashions it produced were for dolls.

Most often the fashion dolls sent out from Paris displayed clothes or jewels. Sometimes, though, the dolls were used to show the elaborate hairstyles women of the time wore.

At first, designers sent their beautifully dressed dolls to women who gave the dolls to their own dressmakers to copy. Later they sent the dolls directly to other fashion designers. These might be in England, or they might be almost anywhere on the continent of Europe.

Much of the trade in dolls was with England. But when war broke out between that country and France, in 1701, the doll trade between the two countries seemed to be ended. That war, the War of the Spanish Succession, lasted for 12 long years.

The British blockaded most of the French coast during that time. They let nothing into that country, and nothing out. There was only one exception. That was the fashion doll.

English ladies longed for them, and those English ladies had a great deal of influence in their country. Many were married to political leaders or other important government figures. No one—especially their husbands—wanted to cross them.

So an agreement was worked out between the ministers of France and England. Between them they arranged for a special pass for these mannequins—these fashion dolls—that permitted them to cross through enemy lines.

That pass was always respected, no matter how bitter the feelings nor how cruelly the war raged.

Not all French dolls went abroad, though. Instead, they were often shipped to the French provinces.

Commerce was so brisk, and so open to deceit, that the government set up a national bureau to control the trade in doll clothes. It made rules and regulations, which usually concerned measurements. In order to prosper, or even to stay in business, tailors and seamstresses had to meet the highest standards.

Although the French were the first to build up this trade in dolls, the English soon copied them. In 1731, a collection was sent to St. Petersburg, the summer home of the czar of Russia. A report in a fashionable journal stated that they were meant to "show the Czarina the manner of dressing at present in fashion among English ladies."

The English sent dolls to India, too, to show women there how to wear English clothes. Until then, the women in Calcutta had worn cloaks on their heads, like mantillas. After the dolls arrived, Indian women draped their cloaks from their shoulders.

More often, though, English dolls went to America. Both New York and Boston received regular shipments. Dolls dressed in sober but up-to-date clothing even went to the Quakers in Philadelphia.

The early French dolls, those that the kings played with, had heads made of wood. They were beautifully carved and just as beautifully painted. But the dolls' bodies were often nothing more than leather bags rolled up tight, and they rarely had legs, although that hardly mattered because the dolls wore long, flowing robes that covered all but their heads and hands.

A few other French dolls had both wooden heads and wooden bodies. More often, though, the bodies were made from bundles of rags, at least for the earlier dolls. Later dolls had bodies of pigskin— white or pink—stuffed with whatever was handy. That might be sawdust; it might be bran.

Still later, dolls had bodies of wood covered with kidskin. This was stretched and pulled and patted until it fit like the proverbial glove.

And French kings continued to send dolls as gifts. In the early part of the 18th century, long after Henry IV sent dolls to his bride-to-be, his

31

descendant, Louis XV, sent a doll to the woman he intended to marry. She was the Infanta of Spain and a descendant of Isabella.

The doll cost over 20,000 livres—many thousands of dollars. It had numerous splendid costumes. To judge from the wardrobes of other such dolls, hers must have included ball dresses for evening wear as well as gowns for daytime. Some were made of rich brocades, a heavy fabric with a design woven into it. Some were made of lace. Others were of fine, light muslin or of sheer gauze.

Her cloak had a matching bonnet, and she had boots as well as shoes. She had nightgowns and shifts and chemises; she had petticoats and dressing gowns. It is probable that the doll had her own bed and her own toilet articles—combs and hairbrushes and mirrors. And certainly, jewels were included.

In spite of this, Louis married a Polish princess, instead of the Infanta. Their son, Louis XVI, married an Austrian princess named Marie Antoinette.

If Isabella of Spain is remembered today for her support of Christopher Columbus, Marie Antoinette is remembered for her role in the French Revolution. She's especially known for her reply when told that the people of France had no bread. "Let them eat cake," she is credited with saying.

Marie Antoinette sent dolls to family and friends alike. These dolls, too, had complete and fashionable wardrobes.

The queen's interest in dolls continued throughout her life. It must have brought her some comfort at the end of it.

Like the king, Marie Antoinette was arrested after the outbreak of the French Revolution. Like the king, she was put to death by guillotine.

Before her death, Marie Antoinette was imprisoned in fortresses that had once been palaces. She spent her time during those terrible days stitching clothes for a small doll that she had brought with her. Some of those clothes have been preserved to this day.

French queen Marie Antoinette made these doll clothes while she was imprisoned during the French Revolution.

PAPER DOLLS

Because fashion dolls were both expensive and difficult to ship, a very practical substitute was found. This was the paper doll, which first appeared in England in 1790.

Then, as now, the flat dolls were made of cardboard or stiffened paper, and their clothes were attached by flaps at the shoulders and sometimes at the sides.

The earliest dolls were about eight inches high, and a doll with its wardrobe cost about 15 cents.

Paper dolls were especially popular toward the end of the 19th century, when many depicted well-known actresses of the time. This is also true today. In America, paper dolls depict stage and screen stars alike. Others have depicted America's political leaders and their families. And, of course, there have been paper dolls that resembled no one in particular but were simply the creations of the artists who drew them.

Paper dolls have been printed in newspapers and magazines, in small booklets and in single sheets. They've been printed and sold in almost every industrialized nation, including the United States, France, Germany, Italy, Spain, and Japan.

An 18th-century English wooden doll.

3

WHAT ARE LITTLE DOLLS MADE OF?

From the beginning of the 15th century—about the time that the French king Charles VI was sending dolls to the English queen—dolls were also being turned out in Germany.

The German dolls were made of wood. That was only natural, because Germany had vast forests. It also had many farmers and peasants who lived in the countryside. These men and women worked in the fields from the time of the spring planting until the crops were harvested in the fall. And they worked from dawn to dusk.

But when winter came and snow covered their fields, they had little to do. It was far too cold to go outdoors. Moreover, because they lived in the countryside, there was almost no place for them to go.

So they took to staying indoors. They sat before their fires and whittled small figures from the wood that was so plentiful. Sometimes these were little animals, but most often they were dolls. Before long, an important industry developed from this modest beginning.

The industry grew and grew. A time came when dolls were no longer made at home but in the factories that sprang up all around.

These German dolls had both bodies and heads made of wood. As time passed, they were exported to nearby countries. By the early part of the 19th century, they were exported to England, too.

But by the 18th century, England too was producing wooden dolls. The most popular— and they were very, very popular—were the peddler dolls, or, as they were sometimes called, "Notion Nannies."

The peddler was always welcome in the small villages of England during that time. Most peddlers were women, and they trudged from one place to another bringing necessary household goods to places where there were few shops. They also brought news and gossip for the lonely housewife. They provided a few minutes of excitement in an otherwise drab and dreary life.

An English peddler doll from about 1830.

Peddler dolls looked almost exactly like the real peddlers. They wore cloaks and bonnets, too, and often had elaborate aprons. They carried trays that they held out over their aprons to display their wares, tiny copies of the goods that real peddlers sold. These could be miniature pots and pans, or equally small brooms or brushes. The peddler doll would have sewing articles, too: the tiniest of scissors, of thimbles, and of packets of needles, along with buttons and buckles and clasps. Perhaps she would have knitting needles and yarns. Perhaps she would have a pair of socks. Almost anything might be on a peddler doll's tray.

Fortune-tellers also roamed the English countryside at that time. Their visits were even more exciting than the visits of the peddlers. Besides bringing news and gossip, they could predict the future through the cards they carried.

Soon fortune-teller dolls appeared in the shops of the small towns. Like the peddler dolls, they were almost always made of wood. In fact, some were actually peddler dolls that carried fortune-telling mottos on their trays. Others had skirts of folded paper in various

This late 18th-century fortune-teller doll has a fortune written on a leaf of her paper skirt.

colors, with a fortune written on each piece. Most were plainly dressed.

One, though, that belonged to England's Queen Victoria when she was just a princess and still a child, had a dress made of silk. But the full skirt was made of folded cards, with a motto on each. One read, "Happy and blest with the man you love best." Another said,

41

"You'll have a boy to bring you joy." The mottos were typical of the times.

This fortune-teller doll was only one of many with which the young princess whiled away long, dreary hours. One day, Victoria would not only be queen of England—and of Ireland, too—but empress of India as well. But at the time, she was still a child, living in a bleak and depressing castle. She found escape from the forbidding atmosphere in her collection of 132 dolls.

All were made of wood and had pointed noses and painted features. They cost so little that they were known as "penny woodens."

Princess Victoria's small wooden dolls were exquisitely dressed in the fashions of the time.

They were small, too. Some were no more than three inches high, while the tallest measured only nine inches. But the princess, with the help of the Baroness Lehzen, who was her governess, made the most wonderful clothes for them.

Some of their outfits were copies of those worn by dancers on stage. Other were copies of the clothes of their favorite actresses in their favorite plays. Still others were copies of the gowns and breeches and coats worn by ladies and gentlemen of the court. No matter what the clothes, though, Victoria and the baroness saw to it that every detail was perfect.

Victoria played with her dolls until she was 14. It was then she put aside such childish pleasures to prepare for the time, three years later, when she would ascend the throne. Today her dolls are in the Victoria and Albert Museum in London.

Although Victoria's dolls were made of wood, at that time, in the first decades of the 19th century, dolls, or at least doll *heads*, were being made of new materials.

One of these "new" materials—wax—was actually very old. It had been used in Italy for figures in crèches from very early times. In other places in Europe it had been used to make effigies—the figures of the dead—that were often a part of funeral services. By 1600, the Germans were making wax dolls that were toys.

In the 19th century, toy dolls with heads and shoulders of wax were made in both England and France. Expensive shops in London, as well as in other large cities, also displayed dolls with heads of fine china, or porcelain, or bisque, newly developed in Europe and much in favor.

A discovery by a young alchemist at the German court of Dresden in 1790 had made possible the manufacture of these materials. His name was Johann Freidrich Boettger, and he succeeded where, for 300 years before him, others had failed.

Throughout that time the Venetians, the Florentines, the French, and the Germans, too, had searched for a formula to make porcelain—or china—as fine as that which came from China itself. Those countries, like England, had large deposits of clay. All used it to make pottery. But whatever they made never matched the china that came from the Orient, either for its delicacy or its beauty.

In 1790, Boettger carried out certain experiments in the laboratory of his master, the Elector Prince Augustus II of Dresden. His goal was to turn clay into gold. He failed at that, of course. But he succeeded in finding the formula for fine porcelain. For a long time after, whatever was made according to his formula was called Dresden china.

Later, when the court moved to Meissen, the china took that name. But whatever it was called, it was used to make small and delicate figures. Before long, these included dolls' heads.

A German doll from about 1838 with a head of wax over papier-mâché.

There were large deposits of clay in France, too, especially near the town of Sèvres. The new process was also used to make china—and dolls' heads—there.

China was also made in the Staffordshire region of England, where there were clay deposits. The English, too, made dolls' heads.

But only those that were glazed are considered true china heads. They have a smooth, glossy

This late 19th-century doll has a china head with molded hair, a cloth body, and leather arms.

surface, which comes from being dipped into a special preparation before the clay heads are baked.

Dolls' heads that were not glazed are known as "bisque." The word is a contraction of biscuit, the technical name for the mixture they're made from. It's called that because it looks so much like unbaked biscuit dough.

Some bisque doll heads are pure white.

A French china-head doll from 1875–1880 with braided hair and a leather body.

A late 19th-century German doll with a bisque head.

Because the color was so much like that of the marble that came from the Greek island of Paros, it was called "Parian."

Dolls with china heads, like those with wax heads, usually had bodies of wood or kid or even stuffed calico. Then, around 1860, dolls appeared that were made entirely of either wax or china. Both, however, had many drawbacks.

Wax dolls, like those of china, were very expensive. Moreover, they developed cracks on the surface as time passed. A wax doll might melt if left too near a heat source; a china doll was easily cracked or broken. Clearly, new materials were needed if dolls were to be both cheaper and longer lasting.

One material, developed in 1820, was called *papier-mâché*, a French term meaning "chewed paper."

Papier-mâché is nothing of the kind, of course. It's merely paper that has been soaked in water until it turns to pulp. After that it's mixed with oils and resins until it's stiff enough to mold. Papier-mâché is very hard when it dries.

At first, papier-mâché was used as a lining under wax heads, to strengthen them. Later it was used alone. In that case, cloth was sometimes used to strengthen the papier-mâché.

Still another material was used to make dolls. At first it was just for their heads. Later it was for the entire doll.

The product was composition, and it was developed in England. For short, it was called "compo." It was a mixture of plaster of Paris, bran, sawdust, and glue, among other things. Like papier-mâché, it could be easily molded when wet. When it dried, it had a hard, long-lasting surface.

But composition wasn't completely satisfactory, either. Dolls made of it were usually painted, then covered with a thin coat of wax. The composition was strong enough, but the wax was still likely to crack. So the search for something better went on.

HOMEMADE DOLLS

Some of the best-loved dolls have been made of some of the most unusual materials. And no one was better at improvising from whatever was at hand than the early American Puritans, who came from England in the 17th century, and later westward-bound pioneers. Even in the most remote parts of the country—even in the wilderness—there was always something handy for making some kind of doll.

One could be made from scraps of calico, the head and body cut from a doubled piece of fabric, then stuffed with more scraps. If there were none, pine needles would do. Arms and legs would be tubes of straight or curved bits of cloth, stuffed and sewn to the body to make them suitably floppy.

A cornhusk doll.

Juice from a crushed berry would provide the color for the facial features. If there was no yarn for the hair, there would be corn silk.

Other dolls might be made from corn husks, folded in half, like cloth, to form the body. It would be stuffed, then tied near one end to form the head. Arms would be made by pulling out a few strands at each side, then tying them back.

Dolls might be fashioned from a bunch of twigs or from an old sock. Buttons could be used for eyes, and the mouth either painted with berry juice or embroidered.

Compared to the fancy dolls found in fine shops, the dolls were certainly crude. But that never mattered to the children who cherished them.

An ancient Greek clay doll with jointed arms,
dating from the fifth century B.C.

WALKING, TALKING DOLLS

Ever since the first dolls were made by primitive people, there have been efforts to make them more lifelike.

The first step was to give them arms and legs that moved. The ancient Egyptians, the Greeks, and the Romans all did that.

A doll found in the ruins of Athens is typical of all three civilizations. It was made of clay, and the head and body were molded in one piece. Each arm and leg, though, was separate. They were attached to the body by a rod that seemed to be screwed into place.

Dolls of this type were also made of wood, especially in Rome. But the skill of making such dolls seems to have disappeared for centuries after the fall of the Roman Empire. In fact, nothing is known about dolls during the Middle Ages, the period between the 5th and 15th centuries.

With the Renaissance, though—with the renewal of culture and civilization that began around the year 1400—dolls reappeared. Among them were jointed dolls, much like those of antiquity. Many had strings attached to their hands and feet, turning them into marionettes. When the strings were jerked, the dolls could be made to dance or to wave their arms.

Puppets were made, too. These were manipulated by a hand inside a hollow cloth body. Puppets and marionettes were a source of amusement to the farmers and peasants who swarmed to see them at local fairs.

But by the end of the 15th century—about the time

54

Columbus discovered America—a new and wondrous type of doll appeared. These were *automatons*, mechanical marvels that would move by themselves when they were wound up. Because they were very expensive, only royalty or the very wealthy could afford them. In the houses and palaces of these people, toy birds were set to flying around and around a room. Or a pair of birds might sit on a perch— or someone's shoulder—and cock their heads in time to music. Dancers could be made to perform stately minuets. A pair of bears might dance together.

One of the finest examples of an automaton was the one Leonardo da Vinci created in 1509. It was a lion, and the great Italian painter made it to honor King Louis XII of France, when the king visited Milan that year.

The king was seated at one end of a huge reception hall when Leonardo entered through a door at the other end. When the Italian master placed the lion on the floor, the beast lumbered across it toward the king. Stopping before him, the lion tore open its chest with its claws in a gesture of respect. At that, the fleur-de-lys, the symbol of the French royal house, fell to the floor at the king's feet.

There is another marvelous example of these automated dolls in the French city of Strasbourg. At the cathedral in that city, they appear before the face of a wonderful clock and strike the hour. The life-size dolls then disappear until it is time to strike the next hour.

Later, in France, other inventors created automatons that were true works of art. In about 1740, Jacques de Vaucanson made a flutist who piped out 12 different tunes. He also made a duck that quacked. When corn was scattered before the bird, it stretched out its neck and gobbled down the kernels.

In 1760, Pierre Jacquet-Droz made a child doll that was said to be able to write. In 1773, his son made one that could

Pierre Jacquet-Droz made this writing doll in 1760.

draw. For the king of Spain, the pair made a sheep that could bleat, as well as a dog that guarded a basket of fruit and barked whenever a piece of fruit was taken from it.

Few automatons were as complex, or as beautiful, as these. Nevertheless, very lovely ones continued to be made until the early part of the 20th century. However, these were never intended as toys for children, not even royal children.

But by the beginning of the 19th century a great many dolls were definitely thought of as playthings. And now designers looked for ways to make their toys automatic. They wanted to make dolls that could walk and talk.

The first person to make a talking doll was a German, Johann Mepomeek Maelzel, who also invented the metronome. The metronome is used even today by musicians to help them keep time as they practice.

Maelzel's doll said two words. When her right arm was raised, she squeaked out "Mama." When her left was raised, she squeaked "Papa."

The doll had a tiny bellows in her body, which was set in motion by a wire attached to the arm. The bellows then produced a column of air that blew across a horn and created a sound.

The doll was displayed at a great Industrial Fair in France in 1823. Three years later, a walking doll was exhibited. She was a mechanical wind-up toy, with springs like those in a watch.

At about the same time, dolls were made that could open and close their eyes. To accomplish this, small lead weights were placed inside the doll's head. The method is still used for dolls today. Eyes that open and close are called sleep eyes.

While dolls were learning to walk and talk and sleep, changes were taking place in their faces and their figures, too. This started when the fashion doll was replaced by fashion engravings and paper dolls in the middle of the 19th century. Because doll makers no longer needed to mold women's heads for dolls, they turned to making those of children.

The very first doll with such a head was made by Augusta Montanari, a celebrated English doll maker. Her husband, Napoleon, was a sculptor in wax, and he worked with her. They had a son, too, who went into the trade, making wax dolls.

Madame Montanari exhibited her first child doll at the famous Crystal Palace Exposition in

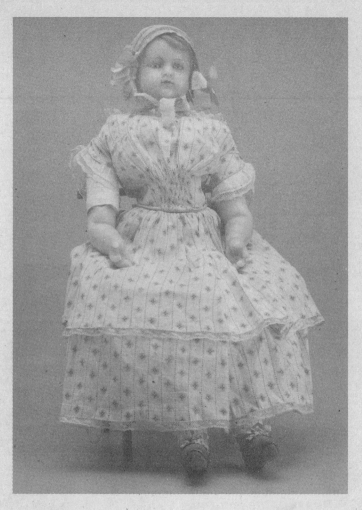

A Montanari doll from 1870. The doll has a wax head, shoulders, and arms, and real hair.

London, in 1851. It won first prize. She exhibited another of her dolls in Paris, at the World Exposition there in 1855. Again her doll won a medal—a first prize.

Eventually Madame Montanari began to make baby dolls, too. Whatever the doll, though—baby or child—it was sure to have a beautiful face with bright cheeks and a tiny rosebud mouth. It was just as certain to be beautifully dressed.

Two doll makers in France soon followed Madame Montanari in making dolls with the heads of children. But they added new devices, too, to make the dolls more lifelike.

Jumeau, the most important dollmaker in that country, developed a means of moving the head of a doll up and down. The head, made of

A doll made by Jumeau, the leading doll manufacturer in France.

bisque or china, could even be moved forward and backward and sideways.

Jumeau also made a number of mechanical dolls that were equipped with music boxes, usually of Swiss make. One such doll holds a bird cage, and when the music begins, the bird flies around the cage, apparently singing, while the doll moves its head from side to side and its free hand up and down. Another musical and mechanical doll, a boy, puts a cigarette between his lips and tilts his head back as if smoking, while his other hand moves back and forth.

Jumeau dolls were exquisitely crafted.

61

The House of Bru was the second most important doll manufacturer in France. Bru dolls were considered very well made, with joints that let them pose in the most natural positions. Monsieur Bru also invented a special mechanism that made it possible for the doll's body to bend forward and backward and sideways.

Madame Bru, the wife of the manufacturer, designed a doll that was far more remarkable. This doll was able to sing a number of different songs, and Madame Bru described her as a "magical talking doll."

Magical singing or talking dolls were made in other places, too. In America, Thomas Edison, who invented both the electric light and the phonograph, placed a very tiny phonograph inside a doll. It played nursery rhymes and songs. When the records were changed, the dolls recited other verses or sang other tunes.

Edison made his doll around 1887, 50 years after the doll that first said "Mama" and "Papa." About 10 years later, a German doll manufacturer introduced a doll like Edison's.

His name was Max Oskar Arnold, and he named the doll "Arnoldia." Arnoldia was large and beautifully dressed in the frilly clothes of the time. Herr Arnold advertised her as "the singing and speaking wonderdoll."

Records for Arnoldia could be had in German, French, or English. They could be specially ordered in other languages, too.

In spite of what seemed to be their many talents, neither of these dolls became popular. Edison's doll was too expensive and only a few

American inventor Thomas Edison made this singing and talking doll around 1887.

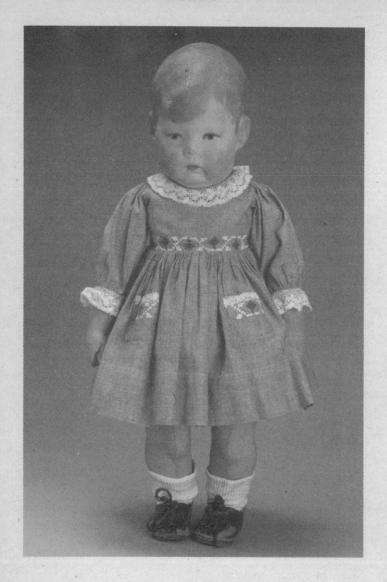

were ever made. Arnoldia was expensive, too. She was made for only three years.

Dolls that endured far longer, and were far more beloved, were those that said only one word. That word was "Mama," and so the dolls were known as "Mama dolls."

These Mama dolls were often inexpensive. Their heads and hands were sometimes of bisque but often of composition. They had cloth bodies stuffed with sawdust or with excelsior or kapok. They had small, simple squeeze boxes in their backs, and spoke when they were leaned foward. In keeping with the tradition begun by Madame Montanari, most of them had pretty faces, idealized rather than realistic.

One of the first to make child dolls that had the faces of real children was Kathe Kruse, a woman who lived in Germany. She began to make dolls around 1910, some 50 years after Madame Montanari began to win medals for her dolls.

This 1922 Kruse doll is made of molded cloth. Its hair and facial features are painted on.

The first doll Frau Kruse ever made was for her own children. She had been searching for a very special doll for them in all the toy shops of Berlin. She knew exactly what she wanted, but no store carried anything remotely like it.

At last, almost desperate, she carved a head from a raw potato. Then she twisted and tied the four corners of a towel, to make arms and legs. When the rest of the towel was filled with sand, it formed the body.

That first doll was crude, certainly. But Frau Kruse kept making dolls. Each was an improvement on the last. As time passed, she replaced the potato heads with heads of molded cloth. The towel bodies gave way to stuffed cloth bodies, like those others also used.

Kathe Kruse held to her goal of making dolls with faces like real children throughout her life. She continued to craft them with the greatest care. Dolls like those made by Kathe Kruse are known as character dolls. Hers are world famous, even today.

In 1899, there was one important new development in dollmaking. It was then that a German named Rudolph Steiner designed a doll that could drink from a bottle. The tiny bottle had an even tinier syphon inside it. That drew the water—or milk—into the doll's head. Afterward, the liquid was emptied into a container under her chair.

This doll, of course, was the forerunner of what would be one of the most popular dolls half a century later.

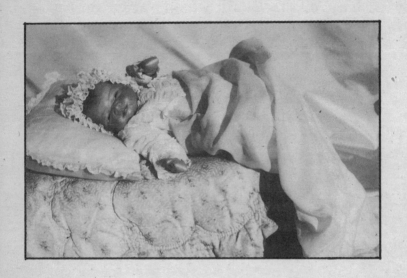

The Bye-Lo Baby, introduced in 1925, was a great success. People were intrigued by the doll's lifelike appearance.

5

BABIES, CHILDREN, AND CELEBRITIES

It was just before the First World War, in the early years of the 20th century, that realistic baby dolls began to appear in toy shops. Several were produced by German firms. Others were made in America. These all sold well. But the most famous and by far the biggest selling baby doll wasn't produced until several years after the war ended. It was the Bye-Lo Baby.

The doll was designed in 1919 by Grace Storey Putnam, the wife of a sculptor. Her model was a three-day-old baby girl Mrs. Putnam found in a Salvation Army hospital.

Mrs. Putnam made a wax model of the little girl's face, then took it from one manufacturer to another. No one, though, was interested in it. All insisted that the doll was too realistic and that it was ugly.

But at last Mrs. Putnam sold the doll to the George Borgfeldt Company in New York. They changed the head slightly, to make it prettier. After they patented the head in 1923, they arranged to have it made in Germany.

The Bye-Lo Baby doll was finally introduced to the American public in 1925. She was an instant success. The fact that the doll's face was that of a newborn child had an immense appeal. There was such a demand for her that buyers lined up outside shops whenever a shipment was received. They even fought to get inside.

The sales of the doll were so great that she came to be called "The Million Dollar Baby." And for many years, Mrs. Putnam earned as much as $70,000 from her annual royalty fees.

With the success of the Bye-Lo Baby, many doll companies made imitations of her. But other companies also made original baby dolls that were different from Mrs. Putnam's. All these baby dolls, though, had one thing in common. All had bent legs, just like the slightly bowed legs of a living baby. This, too, made them seem more real.

Lying on their backs, the new-baby dolls seemed to wave their feet in the air. They could sit up, too. And because of their bent legs, they looked as if they were actually crawling when they were placed on the floor.

One of the best-loved baby dolls to follow the Bye-Lo Baby was the Bubbles doll. Her legs were curved, like those of other baby dolls. Her arms were curved, too.

Bubbles had the face of an infant of about nine months. She already had two teeth and was chubby and happy, with dimples in both cheeks. Her body was of cloth, and there was a voice box tucked inside the body. Because the voice box was superior to those in the earlier dolls, she could say "M a m a" and say it very clearly.

Even more realistic dolls soon appeared. Among them were dolls that were foreshadowed by Steiner's doll that drank from a bottle. There was Baby Tiny Tears, for instance, who not only could drink from a bottle but who shed tiny tears after she'd finished. Another doll that drank from a bottle was the Dydee Doll. A short time after she'd been fed, her wet diapers—or dydees—had to be changed.

Little girls loved their baby dolls, and manufacturers continued to turn them out. Shops sold great numbers of them. But little girls also loved a new doll that they first found beneath their Christmas trees in 1928.

Her name was Patsy, and the Effanbee Company that made her hailed her as completely new and different. While other dolls had the heads of children, Patsy was the first to have the figure of a child, too.

Patsy was made of composition, with molded hair and painted eyes. Her body was modeled after that of a little girl of six or seven. She was slightly plump, with a rounded little tummy and no waist. One of her arms was bent at the elbow. The other was outstretched.

Patsy was the first and the most popular of a family of dolls. Patsy Ann, a larger doll, had sleep eyes which could open and close. The very largest of the dolls was Patsy Mae. She had both sleep eyes and a wig made of human hair.

Smaller dolls included Patsy, Jr., and Wee Patsy, who was only six inches tall. All of these dolls had an impish expression that delighted children. All could turn their heads. Except for Baby Tinyette, a small, bent-legged doll, all could stand alone.

Because of their figures, Patsy and her sisters could wear the sort of clothes that little girls wore. They were sold dressed in party

The Patsy doll family included Patsy, Jr., and Patsyette.

dresses and school dresses, in skirts and sweaters. They were sold in riding clothes and skating costumes. A smaller doll wore a cowboy outfit. There was a boy doll, Skippy, too. He was Patsy's friend, and he might wear short pants or knickers or even a Little Lord Fauntleroy suit.

Some of the finest dolls of this time were created by Beatrice Alexander Behrman, the famous Madame Alexander. She had grown up in New York where her father, a Russian immigrant, owned a toy and doll repair shop. In 1895, he opened the first doll hospital in America.

Beatrice, his eldest child, showed artistic talent even as a child. When she was only 15, she designed her first doll. During the First World War, she helped her father make Red Cross nurse dolls. In 1923, she founded the Alexander Doll Company and began to make unbreakable stuffed dolls.

Many of the Alexander dolls were character dolls. Others were celebrity dolls, modeled after famous people. Child movie stars like Jane Withers and Margaret O'Brien were favorites. So were the young princesses, Elizabeth and Margaret of England. Later, when Elizabeth was crowned as Queen Elizabeth II, Madame

A *Madame Alexander* Alice in Wonderland
doll from 1965.

Alexander made a set of 36 dolls in honor of the
event. They represented all those who took part
in the coronation ceremony.

Among other subjects for dolls, Madame
Alexander chose characters from *Alice in
Wonderland*, *Little Women*, and *Peter Pan*, as
well as *Cinderella* and *Sleeping Beauty*. All her
dolls were so beautifully designed and so
skillfully made that they have become
collectors' items.

SHIRLEY TEMPLE

The most popular of all celebrity dolls, the Shirley Temple doll was also one of the most popular of all dolls. Shirley was created by Bernard Lipfert who, like Madame Alexander, was a famous American designer. The Shirley Temple doll was first sold in 1934. At that time, Shirley Temple, the curly-haired child star, was the darling of America. Each and every film she made was an enormous box-office hit.

The dolls, made of composition, had the same mop of ringlets that the tiny girl did. They had the same dimpled cheeks. And their clothes were copies of those she wore in her movies.

The first doll wore a white dress with either red or blue polka dots. The skirt was full and short. A later doll wore an accordian-pleated party dress, like one that Shirley wore in the movie *Curly Top*. Another doll wore the striped dress that she wore in the same picture. Still another wore the jumper and checked blouse she wore in the movie *Heidi*.

Whatever it was, people snapped up the dolls. More than a million and a half were sold in the six years after the doll was introduced.

A composition Shirley Temple doll from the 1930s wears a copy of the outfit the real Shirley wore in the movie Stand Up and Cheer.

Shirley Temple stopped making movies after nine years. The Ideal Toy Company had already stopped producing the doll. But nearly 20 years later, when television began to show Shirley Temple movies, the company brought out a new Shirley. She was made of vinyl, and she sold as well as the earlier dolls.

Still another version of the doll was brought out in 1975. Like the others, it was a best seller. Like Shirley Temple movies, it was a hit.

Teddy bears have enjoyed a special place of honor in the hearts of children and collectors worldwide.

6

TEDDY AND HIS FRIENDS

Theodore Roosevelt was one of America's most popular presidents. He was a conservationist who worked to preserve the rivers and the forests. He fought against the huge business ventures that took advantage of the little man, and he fought for the rights of the average citizen. He was also a war hero who had led his cavalry company, the Rough Riders, during the Spanish-American War.

Roosevelt had been a frail child, but he grew up to be a great sportsman. He loved to ride and hunt and fish. And he gave his own nickname, "Teddy," to one of the world's best-loved dolls. This is how it came about.

While Roosevelt was president, there was a boundary dispute between two states, Mississippi and Louisiana. In 1902, Roosevelt went to Mississippi to settle the argument. Everyone said that he was "going to draw the line" between the two states.

There was time for recreation, too. Roosevelt used it to hunt bears. But not a single one was sighted, for 10 long days. Roosevelt's hosts were embarrassed by this turn of events. Finally, to save face and to give the president a chance to shoot the bear he'd come after, they captured a cub. They dragged it into camp and then called President Roosevelt.

Roosevelt seized his hunting rifle and dashed from his tent. But when he saw the poor little bear tied to a tree, he turned away in disgust. He "drew the line," he said, at killing such a small and helpless creature.

The story rated headlines in the next day's papers. It even inspired a political cartoon in the *New York Post*. Clifford K. Berryman, a well-known artist, drew the cartoon. In the sketch, Roosevelt turned his back on the terrified little animal. Underneath, Berryman printed, "Drawing the line in Mississippi." Berryman was referring to the boundary dispute and using the story of Roosevelt and the bear to make his point.

The cartoon was printed in newspapers all over the country where it was seen by millions of people. Among them was a Russian immigrant named Morris Michtom. He lived in Brooklyn, New York, where he owned a small toy store.

The original Berryman cartoon.

DRAWING
THE LINE
IN MISSISSIPPI

Sometimes Michtom's wife made stuffed toys to sell in his store. After he saw the cartoon, the two of them put together a little bear made of brown plush. They sewed on buttons for eyes, and then they put it in the window. They placed the Berryman cartoon alongside the bear. Then they made a sign that said "Teddy's Bear." They put that in the window, too.

People were intrigued by the little bear. They stopped to look, and they went into the shop and bought other bears that looked just like it.

After a while Michtom wrote to Roosevelt in the White House and asked permission to call the toy "Teddy's Bear." Roosevelt agreed at once, although he wrote back that he couldn't understand such interest.

Others, though, were just as interested in the bear—and just as enchanted—as Michtom had been. One was a toy importer. He took the cartoon to Germany, where he showed it to a toy manufacturer. Her name was Margaret Steiff, and she was known all through Europe for the stuffed toys made by her company. All were of the highest quality and were sold in the best shops.

The bear that Frau Steiff designed was up to her usual standards. It had a soft coat made of mohair, and the mohair was made from angora

Steiff teddy bears continue to be among children's favorite toys.

goat fur. It was jointed at the shoulders and hips, so that both its arms and legs moved. It had another joint at the neck so that the little bear could turn its head.

The appealing little bear, now called a teddy bear instead of Teddy's Bear, was an instant hit. Manufacturers offered them in every sort of out-fit, from baseball uniform to Rough Rider uni-form. Teddy bears were painted or stenciled on lamps and on tea sets, on children's furniture, even on water pistols.

The craze continued. In England as well as in America, both children and adults carried teddy bears wherever they went. One of these adults was a student at Cambridge, one of England's most prestigious universities. His name was John Betjeman. Years later he would be named poet laureate, his country's official poet.

There is a series of books by the English writer A. A. Milne about his small son, Christopher Robin. The little boy's favorite toy, and his constant companion, is his teddy bear. The bear's name is Winnie-the-Pooh.

The stories Milne told were often true stories of the adventures of his young son and his teddy bear. All have been children's favorites since they were first published.

The books include *Winnie-the-Pooh*, and *The House at Pooh Corner*. They've been translated into every imaginable language. There's even a

Latin version of *Winnie-the-Pooh*. It's called *Winnie Ille Pooh*.

Other books have been written about stuffed toys. One of these was *The Adventures of Two Dutch Dolls*. It told of the travels of two wooden—or "Dutch"—dolls and a rag doll called a Golliwogg.

The Golliwogg (the spelling was later changed to Golliwog) was a black felt doll with wild and wooly black hair. His eyes were bright white buttons, and he had a large, white mouth. He was dressed in a bright red jacket and green trousers. His vest was a bright yellow, and he sported a big bow tie just beneath his chin.

The original doll belonged to a little girl named Florence K. Upton. She was born in New York, although her parents were English. One day, at a fair, she came across the doll. She paid a few cents for it and took it home.

After her father's death, Florence and her mother, Bertha, returned to England. Florence took the Golliwog with her. There, in 1895, she wrote and illustrated *The Adventures of Two Dutch Dolls*, the first book about the stuffed doll.

Other books about the Golliwog followed.

Between 1895 and 1909, one was published almost every year. Bertha Upton wrote these later books, but Florence illustrated them all.

The stories of the Golliwog delighted children throughout England. The doll became such a favorite, in fact, that in 1910 England's largest manufacturer of marmalade began to put his picture on every jar of the confection that was sold. About two years later the first Golliwog dolls were made.

Soon it seemed that everyone wanted one, just as they had wanted teddy bears a short while before. Women bought them and carried them when they went calling or took them with them to tea. Children posed for pictures holding a Golliwog by the hand.

This Golliwog was made around 1960.

The dolls were as popular in America as in England. They were popular in France, too, where Claude Debussy, one of that country's greatest composers, wrote a charming piece of music called *The Golliwog's Cakewalk*. It's part of his *Children's Corner Suite*.

The history of two dolls, Raggedy Ann and Raggedy Andy, is very much like the history of the Golliwog. Just as a real rag doll was the basis for the Golliwog stories, so a real rag doll was the basis of the ever-popular children's book, *The Stories of Raggedy Ann*.

According to one popular legend, Johnny Gruelle, a writer and illustrator, found a tattered doll one day when he was rummaging in the attic of his mother's house. The doll's hair was made of bright red wool, and she had shoe buttons for eyes. When he showed the doll to his mother, he learned that it had been made for her when she was a child.

Shabby though the doll was, Gruelle managed to patch her up. He mended her rips, sewed the button eyes on properly, and touched up her painted face. Soon the doll was as good as new. Gruelle named the doll Raggedy Ann and gave her to his own daughter, Marcella.

87

A picture from Raggedy Ann Stories,
by Johnny Gruelle.

Johnny Gruelle wrote the first book about the doll—there were many to follow—in 1918. To promote sales he displayed the doll alongside copies of it. The promotion worked, and the books sold well. But many people wanted to buy the doll, too. So Gruelle asked his mother and his sister to make some dolls to sell.

Together they made several hundred. They sold them all, but at a loss. There was enough interest in the dolls, though, for commercial manufacturers to arrange to produce them.

Two years later, in 1920, Raggedy Andy joined Raggedy Ann. Both dolls were featured in many subsequent books. Millions of copies have been sold, and these books are now considered children's classics. The dolls are considered classics, too.

Raggedy Ann is still made, just as she was then, with red yarn hair, a painted nose and mouth, and bright round eyes. A heart is painted on her chest, with the words "I love you" written right across it.

The Russian matryoshka doll is actually many dolls that fit one inside the other.

DOLLS AROUND THE WORLD

Many countries have their own special dolls. The country may be one of the African nations, or it may be a land near the Antarctic. The doll itself may be as simple as a bundle of twigs and a bit of cloth. Or it might be as rich and fanciful and lavishly outfitted as some legendary king or queen.

One of the plainest of traditional dolls is the Russian one called *matryoshka*. This is not one doll, though, but many dolls that fit snugly one inside the other.

They are made of wood, and their form is as simple as that of a doll can be. It's nothing more than two balls, not completely round, but more oval in shape. They are of different sizes, with the smaller on top of the larger.

The smaller ball forms the head of the doll; the larger forms her skirt. Together they turn into the Russian peasant women who are called "babushkas." Literally, that word means grandmother. Because grandmothers, at least in Russia, wore kerchiefs on their heads, *babushka* also means a scarf, or kerchief.

These dolls are brightly painted, in brilliant reds and greens and gold, against a background that might be black or simply a natural wood color. Their faces are round and apple-cheeked. Over their skirts they wear white aprons trimmed in bright colors.

The largest doll is often no more than six or seven inches high. She is hollow, of course, and split around the middle. When the two halves are separated, a smaller doll is found inside the larger one. The two dolls are usually identical. A still smaller doll is found inside the second doll. An even smaller one is found inside the third. Only the last doll, the smallest, is carved of solid wood.

In France, there's also a traditional peasant doll. Her name is *Becassine*. She comes from

This Becassine doll has a moveable head, torso, and limbs.

Normandy, a coastal region in the north. Becassine is a stuffed doll and is usually made of felt. She wears a bright green dress and, like the matryoshka dolls, she has a crisp white apron over it. On her head she wears a white kerchief, much like the Russian peasant's babushka.

These dolls can be found in every toy shop, and in sizes from a few inches to a good three feet. They've been the subjects of innumerable children's stories and books. Becassine is such a familiar figure in France that cafés and restaurants are often named for her.

Certain special dolls are very rare and are usually found only in antique shops. There they fetch sky-high prices. These are the "doctor dolls," and they were never toys. Instead, they were used for teaching in medical schools, not only in France but all through Europe.

The earliest of these dolls were made around the year 1500. The latest were made a little after the year 1800. Those were times when no one was allowed to probe into the bodies of people who died to find the cause of death. No one was allowed to use human bodies to teach medical students, either. So dolls were used.

MEDICINE LADIES

For many centuries in China, ladies of high birth owned their own version of doctor dolls. These were often called "medicine ladies."

A wealthy or noble Chinese woman was far too modest to let a doctor examine her. Instead, when she was sick, she sent her servant to him with her medicine lady, marked to show where the pain was. From that he diagnosed her illness and prescribed whatever medicine was needed.

These medicine ladies were often made of ivory. They were posed on large leaves and placed on ebony stands. The nude dolls lay there until there was an illness in the household, and they were sent for.

In England, during the reign of Queen Victoria, dolls were used in much the same way. Ladies then would never think of showing an ankle, let alone a knee, to anyone, even their doctors. So they used dolls to show where the pain was.

Some of these dolls were made of wood, but most were made of ivory. They were beautifully carved, and the chest—and sometimes the stomach—was hinged, so that it could be lifted up. Then all the organs of the human body could be seen inside the body of the doll. All were in their proper places: the heart, the lungs, the liver, the kidneys.

The dolls were practical, of course, and well served their purpose of teaching young doctors anatomy. Many of them were also works of art.

In many countries, dolls were important on happier occasions. One such country was India. One such occasion was a wedding.

For many centuries, weddings could be arranged between the children of important families. Often these children were very young and would not live together until they had grown up. Nevertheless, they were bride and groom, husband and wife.

A suitable gift for the bride? A handsome and expensive doll, decked out in silver.

In some parts of India there is an annual doll festival. It's called the Dassivah Festival and lasts for nine days. During that time little girls dress in their finest clothes while they dress their dolls to look like their parents.

They carry their dolls to the river. When they drop them in, the dolls either sink to the bottom or float out to sea. For the next three months, the children have no dolls to play with.

Some say that this custom began in ancient times, when the dead were thrown into the Ganges, a sacred river. Others believe, though, that the girls were offering their dolls to the goddess who is believed to rule the river.

It is also said that once upon a time live children were sacrificed to the gods, just as once upon a time real slaves were placed in Egyptian tombs. And that just as dolls took the place of those slaves, dolls took the place of the children.

There was a time in Japan, too, when dolls were cast into the rivers. They were supposed to carry away sickness or just bad luck. The Japanese Doll Festival grew out of this custom.

The festival takes place every year on the third day of March. That's about the time when spring begins and when the peach trees first bloom. So sometimes the event is called the Peach-Blossom Festival. During the three days of the festival, Japanese families put their Hina dolls on display.

These are the dolls given to the oldest daughter

Japanese girls play in front of a Hina doll display.

in each family. The first doll is given to the girl when she is born. She is given another doll— sometimes several—on each birthday.

Sometimes there are gifts of miniature furniture, too. There might be a gift of a tiny tea set. Almost anything a doll might need finds its way into the collection.

A complete collection consists of 15 Hina dolls. They are displayed on the five or seven shelves that symbolize a house. Each shelf is covered with a bright red cloth.

A man and his wife are placed on the top shelf. Both are dressed in formal robes copied from those worn by the Japanese nobility hundreds of years ago.

Three dolls are placed on the shelf below. They are dressed in white, with red pantaloons. They represent the serving girls. Each holds a tiny bottle of the traditional Japanese wine, *sake*, along with tiny sake cups.

There are five dolls on the shelf below the serving girls, each a musician of the old Japanese court. In their hands they hold fifes or drums or other ancient musical instruments.

Two dolls called *ziojon* sit on the shelf beneath. They represent the stewards of the household, those men who were in charge of the servants and who oversaw almost everything involved in running a large house. These ziojon hold bows and arrows.

The lowest shelf is for the doll servants. These are called *schicho*, and there are three of them. They hold pails and umbrellas.

In addition to the dolls, there are other tiny objects on display. Miniature lanterns of gold and rice paper flank the dolls. Beside them are the smallest pieces of furniture imaginable: low eating tables, mirror stands, and writing desks.

There are very complicated cere- monies connected with the display of the dolls. Little girls are dressed in their best clothes. They act as hostesses and serve tea and cakes, on the tiniest of plates, in the tini- est of cups, to their parents and friends.

The whole country celebrates the event, too. The fish markets are stocked with the tiniest fish. Bake shops have tiny cakes. There are even miniature vegetables in the markets.

When the festival ends, the dolls are packed away carefully. They will be brought out the next year, in accordance with a custom that dates back for centuries.

The original Barbie was introduced to America in 1959.

8

RECENT DOLLS

What's the most popular doll ever made?

It's Barbie, of course. So far, over 600,000,000 dolls—both Barbie and her family—have been sold. Someone buys a Barbie doll every two seconds.

When Barbie celebrated her 30th birthday in 1989, a gala party was held in her honor at Lincoln Center in New York City. There were books about Barbie and magazine stories, too. Barbie was even featured on the cover of *Smithsonian*, the magazine published by the Smithsonian Institution, the nation's important research and educational center.

When Barbie was introduced in 1959, the doll's manufacturer described her this way: "The Barbie doll: a teenage fashion model! An exciting all-new kind of doll (She's grown-up!) with fashion apparel authentic in every detail ... a miniature wardrobe of fine-fabric fashions: tiny zippers that really zip...coats with luxurious linings...jeweled earrings and necklaces ...There's never been a doll like Barbie."

Barbie was made of vinyl plastic, a material developed just after the First World War. Because it was hardy and inexpensive and waterproof and because it could be easily molded, it was ideal for the factory production of dolls.

Barbie was 11½ inches high, with moveable arms, legs, and head. She had blonde hair that she wore in a ponytail, and she was thin, with a slender waist, like the fashion dolls of a century before.

The idea for the doll came to Ruth Handler, the founder of Mattel, the company that produces Barbie, as she watched her daughter play with paper dolls. Why not a doll with real fabric clothes? she asked herself.

The very first Barbie doll wore a striped bathing suit, sun glasses, pearl-like earrings, and shoes. But there were many other outfits

A 1960 Barbie doll in evening dress.

available. Most of them were influenced by the great Parisian fashion designers of the time, like Christian Dior and Balenciaga. Each outfit had just the right accessories. They ranged from gloves and bags to hair ribbons and jewelry.

There were other dolls, too. They included Ken, Barbie's boyfriend, who was introduced in 1961, and her best friend, Midge, who came along in 1963. Today there are 55 different dolls in the Barbie family. Among them are dolls of almost every race and of many countries.

There have been some small changes made in Barbie over the years. Her smile is different, and so is her complexion. And now her hair is made of a new material, not so soft as it once was. This makes it easier to style Barbie's hair, which is always up-to-date.

Barbie's clothes always reflect the latest trends. When hemlines went way up, Barbie wore mini-skirts. When they went down, Barbie lowered her own.

When girls wore "granny" dresses, Barbie wore them, too. Barbie has also worn the outfits of an airline stewardess and pilot, a doctor, and an aerobics dancer.

106

Barbie's wardrobe has changed over the years. In this photograph, she sports an outfit typical of the 1970s.

Every year, a hundred new outfits are added to Barbie's wardrobe. It now includes 4,000 pairs of shoes and 1,000 handbags.

Nine fashion designers work full-time on Barbie's clothes. Half as many work on the doll's hairstyles. The Mattel Company has used 75 million yards of fabric to make her costumes. Today the company is the fourth largest manufacturer of women's clothing in the United States. And all these clothes are for a doll that's less than a foot high!

The same year that Barbie celebrated her birthday, another doll celebrated one, too. This was G. I. Joe, who was 25 years old.

Joe is a military figure, and the G. I. in his name stands for "government issue." That was the term for all the equipment used by American soldiers from the time of the Second World War. It included his clothes, his rifle, and his backpack, too. Because of this, the name G. I. Joe has come to mean any American soldier. It especially means an enlisted man.

The toy G. I. Joe was the first doll ever made specifically for boys. (The manufacturer, Hasbro, Inc., would rather call him an action figure.) G. I. Joe has also been the most popular. So far, more than 200,000,000 dolls and 100,000,000 vehicles have been sold. G. I. Joe is the most widely collected action figure ever made.

The first G. I. Joe was sold in 1964. He was 11½ inches high, with 21 moveable parts, and he could sit and stand and kneel. He could also assume positions for running, firing, and throwing grenades.

Joe was available in four different uniforms. They were for the army, the navy, the marines, and the air force. He had weapons that were copied from real government issued ones. So were the military vehicles, the jeeps and the tanks, that were sold along with the doll.

During the next few years, new action figures were sold. G. I. Joe was a "fighting man from head to toe," and he was joined by fighting men from other countries. There were British, Russian, German, Australian, French, and Japanese soldiers to battle along with Joe.

G. I. Joe was first introduced in 1964.

109

And Joe changed, too. Talking figures came along in 1968. In 1974 a doll with a "Kung Fu" hand grip was added. A later doll had moveable eyes.

Although the doll was among the best-selling top 10 toys each year, the manufacturer, Hasbro, had to stop making it in 1978. The reason was its cost.

G. I. Joe was made of plastic, and plastic was made from petroleum. An international oil crisis that year made petroleum so expensive that Hasbro could no longer afford to make the toy. They did make an announcement, though. "G. I. Joe," they said, "has been furloughed."

But G. I. Joe was back in 1982 and introduced as "A Real American Hero." This figure was smaller than the original doll. Now he was only 3¾ inches high.

He was also part of a team, leading 16 other dolls. These were the "good guys." There was another team, also numbering 17 dolls. They were the "bad guys." Each side had new weapons, and there were new vehicles, too. Today, G. I. Joe is sold around the world.

The year that G. I. Joe came back was the year that people all over America went wild over the Cabbage Patch Kids. These were cloth dolls, about two feet high. Their arms and legs were short and pudgy. They were dough-faced, with round, fat cheeks, and no chin. Often they were cross-eyed, too. And one out of three was a boy.

Many people thought the dolls were ugly. Yet it seemed that every child wanted one. Some people waited in line for 14 hours in order to get a doll at Christmastime. Others screamed and elbowed and pushed. That year, 2,500,000 Cabbage Patch Kids were sold.

The first dolls were actually made about six years earlier, in 1977, by Xavier Roberts. He was an art student still in college in Cleveland,

America fell in love with Cabbage Patch dolls.

Georgia. One of the courses he took was in soft sculpture. He used that technique to make the dolls that he called "Little People." They were handcrafted, and prices for them ranged from $125 to over $1,000.

Roberts made believe that he didn't really sell the dolls. Instead, the dolls were supposedly adopted by the people who paid for them and took them home.

The dolls were made and displayed in a building that had once been a clinic. Roberts re-named it the "Babyland General Hospital." He had his salespeople dress in nurses' uniforms and doctors' white coats.

Each doll was different, and each had a name. No two names were alike. Each doll had a birth certificate, too, as well as adoption papers. Roberts even insisted that those who "adopted" his dolls take an oath, swearing to take care of them forever.

A few years later, Roberts sold the rights to make the doll to Coleco, a company that made computers. Now the dolls were mass-produced, rather than handcrafted. But Coleco used new computer technologies to make each doll different from all the others. They made some dolls with freckles, others without. They made dolls with long hair and dolls with short hair and dolls with no hair at all. The differences were small, but they were important.

Just like Roberts, Coleco gave each doll a name. Just like him, they packed adoption papers with each doll. Like him, they asked every owner to take an adoption oath.

For two years, people fought for the Cabbage Patch Kids. And then they simply stopped buying them. The craze was over, and the company was bankrupt.

Cabbage Patch Kids are still being made. But now they're made by Hasbro, the company that makes G. I. Joe. They make only a few, compared to the number made by Coleco.

Meanwhile, other new dolls are being introduced every year. Among the latest are those that not only cry but laugh, too. There's now a doll with hair that appears to grow back after it's cut. Another doll makes sucking noises.

There's a doll named Teddy Ruxpin that

moves his lips and rolls his eyes while he tells stories. (A battery-operated cassette under his fur controls this.) For one season, he was a best-selling toy. Now he's almost forgotten, although he's still manufactured. A doll named Chatty Cathy had been introduced years before. She had a tiny battery-operated phonograph inside and could utter 16 phrases. Among them were "I love you, Mommy," and "When's my birthday?" She, too, is now almost forgotten (except by collectors, who love her).

Other dolls have come and gone, too. Among them have been the Flower Kids, which look very much like the Cabbage Patch Kids, and a doll called Cheerful Tearful.

And more dolls will come. Some will capture the hearts of little girls and boys. Others will be ignored by them.

But some doll, of some type or other, will soothe and comfort, will delight and amuse children throughout the world. The dolls will be bathed and fed and dressed and cradled and rocked and lulled to sleep for centuries to come, as they have been for centuries past.

GLOSSARY

Automatons: Mechanical dolls that move by themselves when wound up.

Becassine: A traditional French peasant doll.

Bisque: Unglazed china, used as a material for dolls' heads.

Composition: A mixture of plaster of Paris, bran, sawdust, glue, and other materials used to make doll heads and, later, entire bodies.

Crèche: A group of figures representing the Nativity, the birth of Jesus Christ.

Daruma doll: A Japanese doll named for the Buddhist priest Daruma, weighted so that it cannot fall over.

Dassivah Festival: The annual doll festival in India.

Doctor dolls: Dolls used between the years 1500 and 1800 for teaching in medical schools throughout Europe.

Fortune-teller dolls: 18th-century English wooden dolls made to look like real fortune tellers.

Grande Pandore: A 17th-century French fashion doll.

116

GLOSSARY

Hina dolls: Dolls given to the oldest daughter in a Japanese family and put on display during the annual Japanese Doll Festival.

Kachina: A spirit worshiped by the Hopi Indians; also, a figurine representing that spirit.

Marionette: A jointed doll with strings attached to its hands and feet.

Matryoshka: Brightly painted Russian dolls that fit one inside another.

Medicine ladies: Dolls used for many centuries by wealthy Chinese women to indicate illnesses to their doctors.

Papier-mâché: A material made from paper pulp that is used to make dolls' heads.

Peddler dolls: Wooden dolls, made in England beginning in the 18th century, that looked just like real peddlers.

Petite Pandore: A 17th-century French fashion doll that modeled ladies' underwear.

Sleep eyes: Dolls' eyes that open and close by means of small weights placed inside the doll's head.

Tilting doll: Chinese doll inspired by Buddha, weighted so that it cannot fall over.

Ushabti: Dolls placed by Egyptians in the tombs of people who had died.

INDEX

119

ABOUT THE CONTRIBUTORS

VIVIAN WERNER is a professional writer with more than 25 years experience in writing and editing. She has published 44 books in many fields, including novels, biographies, and young adult and children's fiction and nonfiction. She lives in New Haven, Connecticut.

JULIE DURRELL attended Skidmore College and Pratt Institute, and has illustrated a number of children's books. She lives in Greenwich, Connecticut.

REBEKAH MONTGOMERY, consultant, is the editor of *International Doll World*, a magazine for doll collectors.

PHOTO CREDITS